The Love Feast

BY: JOHN D. RITCHESON

APRIL 2009

The Love Feast

Published by:
Intermedia Publishing Group
P.O. Box 2825
Peoria, Arizona 85380
www.intermediapub.com

ISBN #9780982045879

Copyright by Thomas Nelson Inc.
All Scripture quotations, unless otherwise indicated, are taken from the King James Version.
"The Love of God" written by Frederick M. Lehman; published in Songs That Are Different, Volume 2, 1919. Used by permission.
All rights reserved.

Printed in the United States of America by
Epic Print Solutions

No part of this publication may be reproduced, stored in a retrieval system, or transmitted in any form or by any means - electronic, mechanical, digital photocopy, recording, or any other without the prior permission of the publisher.

This book is a must read for all those who are in search of a love that reaches beyond that which is human, limited, and inadequate. John in his ministry and life has exemplified God's love in action. Now in his own passionate style, he has done a great job capturing and displaying the essence of this love for all those who crave to experience the difference.

Dr. Darrell Bewley
Shelby St. Church of God

Evangelist John Ritcheson is an example of God's love in action. Love is the most powerful weapon we can use to win our families, friends and communities over to Jesus. Since "love never fails" we need to gain a greater understanding on this subject. Evangelist John Ritcheson is definitely the man of the hour that God has raised up to teach us how to walk in God's love. I've seen God's love operate in John's life melting the hearts of the hardest cases, bringing them to a place of repentance. If we are going to be effective in changing our generation, we must learn what love is and how to walk in it.

Pastor Marco Garcia
The Way World Outreach Ministries

John Ritcheson tells the powerful truth of God's love in an impactful and moving way. His passion for God is evident and his compassion for God's children is obvious. This is a book about God's miraculous love that is poignant and timely for the Body of Christ. It is an encouraging tool of inspiration that will bring anyone into closer communion with God. You will be drawn into the very arms of God as you read this book. John, thank you for allowing God to speak through you and for touching my heart.

Michael Chitwood
General Overseer
International Congress of Churches & Ministers

John Ritcheson knows about God's love. Maybe in a way that very few can explain. I can think of no one more qualified to try and describe the indescribable and capture in words that which cannot quite be contained by human understanding. John will come as close to it as any author you will read because he has personally experienced God's love for himself. The redemption road for John led to the cross and from there he has taken a world-wide journey of ministry and modeled God's love as a faithful husband, father, friend and minister.

This new book reminds me of the words scribbled on the wall of a prison cell, found after the death of the inmate. It became one of America's favorite hymns:

"Could we with ink the ocean fill,
And were the skies of parchment made;
Were ev'ry stalk on earth a quill,
And ev'ry man a scribe by trade;
To write the love of God above
Would drain the ocean dry;
Nor could the scroll contain the whole;
Tho, stretched from sky to sky.
O Love of God, how rich and pure!
How measureless and strong!
It shall forevermore endure,
The saints and angels' song."

Tim Hill
General Assistant Overseer
Churches of God International

John Ritcheson understands the miracle of the unconditional love of God probably better that anyone else that I know. His entire life's work as an evangelist is based around sharing this amazing gift with the world, sacrificing his time, treasures and talents to ensure that as many people as possible have the opportunity to experience that same unconditional love of God that he does.

Overcoming unbelievable odds and excelling in spreading the gospel, John has not only been a blessing to me and to my church, but I am privileged to call him one of my best friends. His ability to connect with people on a personal level is unparalleled, and he willingly shares his heart with each and every word that he preaches or writes.

By taking this message of love directly to those people who need to hear it most, John follows in the footsteps of Christ, and is a role model for Christians everywhere.

Pastor Ronnie Hepperly
Restoration International Outreach

John Ritcheson is absolutely one of the greatest examples of what God can do I have ever met. To hear him preach is always an experience that demands one to move higher in their walk with God. John's teaching on the love of God is done with passion and reality in such a way that everyone realizes God loves them. I have personally worked with John for the past 14 years and can tell you from experience that you will be blessed by this book. I highly recommend you to read with openness to God this book and allow Him to take you to a higher plain. This is a must read for the person who truly wants to reach their potential in their purpose.

Pastor George Moxley
Unity Church of God

Of all of the people with whom I am acquainted, no one is more qualified to write about the love of God than John Ritcheson. I have known this passionate evangelist for more than two decades. His life and ministry are consumed with winning the lost to Jesus Christ by revealing God's love to all people. A man of stalwart integrity, John Ritcheson is an example of a life transformed by the power of the Cross, the greatest example of the love of God. It is with pleasure I recommend this book and the ministry of John D. Ritcheson.

Raymond D. Hodge, D. Min.
Administrative Coordinator
Tennessee Church of God State Executive Offices

FOREWORD

When I think of my friend Bishop John D. Ritcheson, two images spring to mind. I see him first as one of the most energetic, enthusiastic worshipers and preachers of the gospel I have ever known. Second, I recognize the central heart that motivates his pulpit ministry the love of God.

For much of his 27 years of preaching ministry, Bishop Ritcheson and I have been friends and coworkers. Because we share the same perspective on ministry, it has been comfortable for me to work with him. We both understand that ministry is empty and fruitless unless it is anointed by the Spirit of God, and if it has His anointing, it produces results: changed lives, redeemed souls, healed bodies, supernatural miracles.

Bishop Ritcheson serves as a member of the Board of Governors of the National Bible College and Seminary and on the Board of Executive Elders of the T.L. Lowery Global Foundation. He lends his considerable influence to the effectiveness of both institutions.

I share the outlook, expressed in this book, about the tremendous need that exists in our culture for an awareness by men and women of the love of God. People's whole lives are radically altered when they grasp the deep truth that they are the personal objects of God's loving care.

I commend The Love Feast and pray God's blessings upon you as you read it. I borrow Paul's meaningful and heartfelt prayer and lift it up to God on your behalf: "That Christ may dwell in your hearts by faith; that ye, being rooted and grounded in love, may be able to comprehend with all saints what is the breadth, and length, and depth, and height; and to know the love of Christ, which passeth knowledge, that ye might be filled with all the fullness of God" (Ephesians 3:17-19).

T.L. Lowery, Founder
T.L. Lowery Global Foundation

Dedication

This book is dedicated to all the wonderful people and pastors that I have met in churches all over this country who have expressed God's love to my family and me over these past several years. I could never find the words to express my heartfelt gratitude to all of you. I am dedicating this book to my Master, Jesus, and all of His children who have overwhelmed me with their love over the years. Thank you for being vessels of our God's love.

In His Service,
John D. Ritcheson

Introduction

For months now, God has been dealing with me to write a book on His perfect love. God is the most misunderstood individual in the universe. God is not a God of judgment, although He will judge all someday, but He is a God of mercy and love. His love is the only thing greater than His power.

I feel compelled to write this book because no one should go through life without realizing they are loved by someone so deeply that He would give anything for them. God passionately loves you. You may ask how I know this.

First of all, I have had a relationship with God for greater than 28 years and something that always stands out to me about God is, His love for me.

Secondly, His Word (which cannot lie) tells us this is true.

In the Book of John, 3:16 tells us that: *For God so loved the world that He gave His only begotten Son, that whosoever believeth in Him should not perish, but have everlasting life.*

Most of you know that God gave His Son to die on the cross for the sins of all men everywhere. How much more could He love you?

I am a father and I believe those who know me best, would say that I am a loving person who loves his family and I am someone who would die for my family, the church, and for God. One would never really know that unless placed in a position to have to make that choice, but in my heart, I believe I would lay down my life for my family, the church and for God.

In saying that, I feel that I could not give my son John to be crucified in your place or in mine. However, this is what the Father did for you and me. That is love!

In my travels, I am surprised, shocked and saddened to see how many people really believe that no one loves them. Nothing can be farther from the truth because the greatest person of all loves them – God.

You may wonder why people don't believe they are loved. I believe there are a few reasons.

First, many people don't know what pure, real true love is because to many people, it is just lust or feelings. That is why they fall in and out of "love" all the time. Love is a verb or action. Love is doing and enduring.

Secondly, we live in a dysfunctional society where fathers and mothers can just walk away from their children, while others stay with their children, but are abusive to them.

It hurts me so much to realize as I write this that there are many who have difficulty receiving the Father's love because their earthly father abused them sexually, physically and/or mentally.

God's love is a pure love. You might ask if God is so loving, why would He allow those who abuse others to live? That is not a simple one-answer question, but it is proof of God's love and He wants to give the abusers a chance to repent. However, if they do not repent, then *"vengeance is mine, saith the Lord, I will repay."*

Always remember, with all people as with us, God would rather forgive than punish. He is longsuffering.

I want you to know that God loves you and so do I. I believe and pray that God will reveal His love to you in "The Love Feast." I pray His love will become a reality to you as you read it.

Table of Contents

Endless Love - Chapter 1 1

Love vs. Fear - Chapter 2 7

What Is Fear - Chapter 3 13

God's Perfect Love - Chapter 4 17

Where Does Fear Come From? - Chapter 5 23

Who Am I? - Chapter 6 27

The Blessing - Chapter 7 33

Pronouncing The Blessing - Chapter 8 49

Taking Control - Chapter 9 63

It's For You! - Chapter 10 67

Special Thank You 82

Endless Love
Chapter 1

While wondering where to begin this journey into God's love with you, I look around me and I find myself on Jekyll Island in Georgia. It is called Georgia's Jewel and I understand why, because it is indeed a wonderful place.

I would like to give special thanks to Brother Harris and all the wonderful people at Bay Harbor Church of God for providing this place for me to stay so I could write this book. This place has truly inspired me.

This Thursday in April, there are not many guests on the Island. The atmosphere is very quiet and peaceful, as is God's presence. All I can hear are the waves softly pounding on the beach, the birds singing and the winds gently blowing through the giant water oaks.

As I look out a large window in my room, I can feel God's love even as I write this. I am to the point of tears while looking out over the ocean at God's beautiful creations.

I can see the blue sky of a cloudless day. I can see dolphins playing in the waves and pelicans diving from the sky looking for an evening snack. Seagulls fill the shoreline. Off in the distance, I can see shrimp boats filling their nets.

As I look at it all, I am in awe of its vastness and that is when it strikes me that this is where to start this book. God's love for you is endless, as vast as the oceans. You may think I am just getting caught up in the moment, but you're wrong and I believe God's Word will back me on this.

Romans 8:35-39 says:

35. Who shall separate us from the love of Christ? Shall tribulation, or distress, or persecution, or famine, or nakedness, or peril, or sword?

36. As it is written, For thy sake we are killed all the day long; we are accounted as sheep for the slaughter.

37. Nay, in all these things we are more than conquerors through him that loved us.

38. For I am persuaded, that neither death, nor life, nor angels, nor principalities, nor powers, nor things present, nor things to come,

39. Nor height, nor depth, nor any other creature,

shall be able to separate us from the love of God, which is in Christ Jesus our Lord.

Notice verses 38 and 39 – "*I am persuaded,*" meaning: to know without a shadow of a doubt.

Before I go any further, I want you to know I am persuaded; I am a witness of God's love. If I die, I die into His love.

For some, life is so painful that they would prefer death, but God says no matter what life brings you, My love will get you through whatever it is.

In this passage, the word "*angels,*" must be referring to fallen angels, because God's angels would never try to keep you from God's love.

The devil is a fallen angel, but he can't keep God's love away from you.

"*Principalities,*" - demonic beings, can't keep God's love away from you.

"*Nor powers,*" - all the power that be, can't keep God's love away from you.

"*Nor things present,*" - whatever you are currently going through including your failures, can't stop God's love from reaching you.

"*Nor things to come*" – that means; I can make

it because my tomorrow is full of God's love no matter what comes my way. God's love will see me through, oh yes, it certainly will. He has brought me through countless times.

"*Nor height,*" - that includes outer space, because God's love for you is bigger than the cosmos.

"*Nor depth,*" - because God's love for you is deeper than the deepest part of the ocean.

"*Nor any other creature*" – no one, NOTHING can keep you from the love of God.

You may think you are awful and that you have stopped God from loving you, but you haven't because it says in this passage of scripture that "*nothing shall be able to separate you from the love of God.*"

I want to tell you and the whole world – anyone who will listen – about the vastness of His love because Romans 8 declares that God's love can reach me no matter how low I've gone. He can reach me even if I have a mountain of sin as high as the Heavens themselves. God can reach me no matter what my circumstances are or where I am.

You may be thinking that it is easy for me to say because I am a preacher. You are right, but I wasn't always a preacher. I was a drug addict and an alcoholic, but God came to me and He will come to you through Christ Jesus. His love has already been provided for you through Christ Jesus; please receive that love now, if you haven't already.

Ask God into your heart and simply ask for forgiveness of your sins and for Jesus to come into your life as Lord and Savior. He has already paid for your forgiveness on the cross so you might as well receive it.

Simply ask for it by faith and you will feel His love. It's already there. You may not feel it because you aren't opening yourself up to His love. He loves you so much, but He will not force his love on anyone.

Would you like to receive His love right now? If you would, please pray this with me, "Father, please forgive me a sinner. I know you want to because Jesus died for me on the cross and He rose from the dead and He now sits at your right hand. Jesus, I ask you now to come into my life as my Lord and Savior. In Jesus name amen."

If you have done that before, or for the first time just now, that prayer makes you a child of God – no arguments. "*Nothing can separate you from the love of*

God in Christ Jesus my Lord."

The next chapter in this book will tell you more about His endless, perfect love.

Love vs. Fear
Chapter 2

Not only is God's love endless, it is perfect as well. This fact is very important because we live in fearful times. The Bible said the last days would be perilous times. There are many elements producing these fears:

1. Lack of Spirituality in This Country

    If everyone knew God, they would know that God is in control and that would eliminate fear because we also would realize how much He loves us.

2. Terrorism

    Terrorism is an ever present threat with the war in Afghanistan and Iraq and the possibility of nuclear conflict with Iran and/or North Korea are always imminent.

3. The Economy

    How high will gas prices go?

4. The Weather

The problems in nature, the hurricanes in 2004 and 2005, Mount Saint Helens, the Tsunamis, etc. There are a lot of things in the natural that could make you fearful if you didn't trust God with your future.

I'm not suggesting that you become an ostrich and stick your head in the sand, that's not at all what I suggest.

However, I do not fear my future because I know who holds my future – an all loving God. In fact, I don't fear my past because Jesus was Jesus yesterday. I don't fear my present because Jesus is Jesus today. I don't fear my future because Jesus will be Jesus forever – "*the same yesterday, today and forever.*"

I talk to a lot of people in my travels who describe to me what can only be called a spirit of fear. To combat this, we need the sword of the spirit, a <u>word</u> <u>from</u> <u>God</u>. I have a Rhema Word from God for you.

Ephesians 6:17 reads like this: "*And take the*

helmet of salvation, and the sword of the Spirit, which is the Word of God."

There are two words translated "word" in the Bible. They are: Logos, which means: written, which is powerful and produces seed faith. It has to grow in you to produce the miracles.

In this verse, however, the word is Rhema which is a spoken word from God. It can come to you as a small, still voice through a sermon, a song, as you study the Bible or a book, but the Word jumps on you and you know you've heard from God about your problem – that's a Rhema Word, but don't stop there. Let the Holy Ghost finish what He started. It is the Spirit's sword when God gives you a Rhema Word. Speak it in prayer about that problem and every time you do, you become the sword of the Spirit in the hand of the Holy Ghost as you yield. Isn't that awesome?

I believe this book is a Rhema Word from God, not just to the church, but to the entire world. We all want to be loved and we are.

Before I go any further, I must say to those who

battle fear "please don't feel condemned." I have battled a spirit of fear too. My most prominent fear was the fear of failure – failing God, failing the church and failure to minister effectively.

I've feared losing my health, but not death. I've seen both sides and Jesus is on both sides. So if I live, I live in Christ, if I die, I die in Christ. He is on both sides of the fence, so I don't fear dying, but I do fear what my family would do if I couldn't work.

I have feared rejection. Does this sound familiar? I know fear is no laughing matter, but I know the cure for fear – the love of God.

My daughter battled a spirit of fear. She was living closer to God than ever, but still had the fear that she wasn't good enough for God to love. I knew that was a lie of the devil. I could tell her it was an attack, but she needed to know what to do about it. So you know, I sought God long and hard and God gave me this book for her, and now for you.

That's how this book was born. I spoke this to her and prayed it over her and it set her free almost instantly.

It is my prayer that this book will help you also find freedom from fear.

What Is Fear: Chapter 3

In order to deal with fear, we must understand what fear is. We know it can paralyze us, but what is it and why is it so dangerous? There are several definitions – both spiritual and physical. Let's start with the spiritual.

First of all, fear and faith are the same thing, both are a belief in something that cannot be seen, is going to happen. What you believe long enough, you will receive.

Job said, "*What I believed (or feared) has happened to me.*" Faith in God is progressive and fear is faith in reverse. It will take you backwards. Fear is faith in what the devil says. Faith believes what God says. Do you see why fear is devastating spiritually?

The good news is that God is not a God of fear, but of love and His love is available to all by faith.

Physically, the number one factor for a long life and good health is the state of your mind and emotions.

Fear has a devastating effect on both of the leading causes of death in women – cancer and heart disease.

Fear causes low self-esteem which can cause all kinds of bad things to happen to a woman's body chemistry. Low self-esteem is a result of fear – the fear of being too fat, not being a good mom, not being a good wife, etc. Guys, if you want your wife to be physically healthy, she must be emotionally healthy. Talk positively to her about herself and it will do wonders for her self-esteem.

Finally, when we are in danger, our body releases adrenaline which causes an acute stress response called flight or fight. This is great if you have to outrun a train or fight an attacker, but when fear unnecessarily enters your body, your body kicks into flight or fight and if this continues over a long period of time, it can result in high blood pressure and an irregular heart beat as well as many other possible health problems.

We are so wonderfully made by God that when a fearful thing happens such as an accident or an attack, we can respond with great power, but our bodies are only meant to be in this state for a short period of time, for emergencies.

If one stays in the state of fear for longer periods of time, it can literally cause premature death. But not to worry – God has an answer to all the fears of life – His perfect love. Let's examine His perfect love in Chapter 4.

God's Perfect Love
Chapter 4

I John 4:18 *"There is no fear in love; but perfect love casteth out fear: because fear hath torment. He that feareth is not made perfect in love."*

Perfect love, God's love, is not man's love. God's ways are not man's ways. God doesn't fall in and out of love with you like people do. When God says He loves you, He does so with a perfect love. Hasn't he proved it? God's love surpasses all human understanding.

We must begin to realize, as hard as it may seem, that you and I exist to be loved by God and to love God in return. It is a spiritual love that is to last for all eternity. It brings complete mental and emotional wellness which is not possible without God's love relationship in our lives.

The word <u>perfect</u> here means complete perfection which implies it is from someone who is perfect and we know the only one that can be is God, for He is the only one that is perfect.

The word love is <u>agape</u>, meaning to have great affection toward you. It also means benevolence and that you are dear to Him. It suggests the title of this book, "The love feast" where we feast on God's love. That is His desire for us. Do you see why this kind of love casts out all fear?

When you are fearful, just feast on God's love. One of the fruits of the Spirit is love. Dine on the fruit of His love through the Holy Spirit. *"Come and dine the Master calleth, come and dine."*

You might ask where fear comes from. It comes from one of three places:

1. It can come from circumstances that are usually temporary such as a bad report from a doctor or losing your job, etc.

2. It also can come from incorrect teaching. Some people have used the word fear to control people. There is a fine line between leading a church or people and controlling them.

3. Misunderstanding what you are being

taught is an example of this.

Most of us got saved out of fear – a fear of hell, of God's judgment or missing the rapture. This is a good thing because the beginning of wisdom is the fear of God, not to live in fear of God, but to know you must repent of sin to be forgiven of sin. The fear of God's judgment brings us to repentance; but once you are saved, you are a member of God's family and as a baby Christian, you must grow in God to perfection.

You got saved out of fear, but you can only grow in God through love. You can only grow through relationship. How or why would you spend time with someone you fear?

Remember I John 4:18 "*He that feareth is not made perfect in love.*" So, when it is circumstantial or bad teaching, then where does fear come from? Stinking thinking or bad thinking.

In dealing with the things we control, there is another in which I will deal with in detail in the next chapter. I realize we often cannot control what happens to us, but we can control how we respond. Now back to bad thinking.

I believe it is a sense of inferiority and bad thinking when we ask "why would God love me?" We often think this particularly when we are trying to live close to God which we all should be doing. The closer you get to God, the more sensitive you become to every little thing that does not please Him. Then when you do not please Him, you ask for forgiveness, then, you go on in love.

Remember, you are a work in progress. He's the potter and you are the clay. Always remember, God is the author and finisher of your faith. He finishes what He starts.

When God sees you He sees the glorified you. As any artist, He sees the finished work in the clay. I want to impress one more thing upon you before we go on to where fear comes from… never fall into thinking that God loves you for what you do. No, no, a thousand times no.

God loved you before you got saved. He did not love you less then nor does he love you more now. We know that *no greater love has a man than to lay down His life for a friend*, but while I was yet a sinner, God laid down His life for me.

The father loved me so much that He gave His Son; His Son gave His life out of love before I got saved. He loved me during my vilest sin.

I know that in trying to live right, I may not be perfect, but I love a perfect God. What makes me think He doesn't love me? Stinking thinking, that's what.

God loves you – the good, the bad and the ugly. He loves you too much to leave all the junk in your life and so He convicts and even punishes, but always to perfect you in love. You cannot be made perfect through Him except through love.

Now for the question, "from whom does fear come?" It would not do any good to rebuke something if it is from God.

Where Does Fear Come From?
Chapter 5

II Timothy 1:7 says: *"For God hath not given us the spirit of fear; but of power, and of love, and of a sound mind."* First, we learned that God did not give us fear. It didn't come from God. Also, we learned that there is a spirit of fear. I know God is referring to the Spirit of the Holy Ghost as love, but I also know for a fact that there are demons that specialize in fear; usually it will hit you out of nowhere.

The good news is that whether it is circumstances, bad teaching, stinking thinking or demonic forces, the perfect love of God casts it out. Praise God forever!

Now why is Timothy so fearful? Because Timothy is struggling, that's why. He is backsliding, not a sinner, but backing up from God. You see saints, we all have failed God and we are of the belief that God doesn't love us anymore and we deserve fear.

But Paul, in II Timothy 1:6 said this to Timothy when he was failing God: "*Wherefore I put thee in remembrance that thou stir up the gift of God, which is in thee, by the putting on of my hands.*" Timothy wasn't using his gift. I believe it was the gift to preach effectively.

No man can give you your anointing, but they can impart the Spirit as well as giftings. Peter and John laid hands on people to receive the Holy Ghost and Elijah's mantle fell on Elisha.

Timothy is fearful because he wasn't preaching. Why wasn't he preaching? Look at verse 8: "*Be not thou therefore ashamed of the testimony of our Lord, nor of me his prisoner; but be thou partaker of the afflictions of the gospel according to the power of God.*" Timothy had become ashamed of the testimony of the Lord.

He saw that Paul was about to be put to death and no doubt he thought that if it could happen to a great man like Paul, it could happen to him.

So, in his backup or defense, denying the Lord to some extent, Paul said don't be ashamed of the Lord or me.

He is in trouble now. He has good reason to fear. In the middle of this, Paul writes that God didn't give you fear, son, but He did give you some stuff and even when you're struggling, you need to know this.

God gave us power! Notice that Paul said, "*He didn't give us*," not just for Timothy, but also Paul, you and me.

The word power here means miraculous power, abundance of ability and might, miracle working power and God's strength. Why would God do this? He also gave us love – agape love, perfect love, "The love feast" which produces a sound mind.

Sound and mind are the same word here. Why would He repeat himself like that? Because He wants us to get it, to understand that the word means self control and discipline, to make you a disciple through correct thinking.

What is correct thinking? That God loves you! Why would He love me like that? You wouldn't ask that if you knew who you were in Christ.

Who Am I?
Chapter 6

There is an identity crisis in the church today in the body of Christ. Romans 8:14-17 says:

14. For as many as are led by the Spirit of God, they are the sons of God.

15. For ye have not received the spirit of bondage again to fear, but ye have received the Spirit of adoption, whereby we cry, Abba, Father.

16. The Spirit itself beareth witness with our spirit, that we are the children of God:

17. And if children, then heirs; heirs of God, and joint-heirs with Christ; if so be that we suffer with Him, that we may be also glorified together.

You are a child of God now that you are born again. You are not born in this world a child of God, even though He loves you. You must be born again by spiritual adoption. By asking Christ into your heart, as your Lord and Savior, you become His child.

When someone adopts a child, they choose that child. Oh saints, that makes it even more wonderful. God chose us with our faults, our weaknesses and our baggage. Isn't God wonderful?

I am going to share with you what I feel is one of my biggest failures since I've been saved. It happened a few years ago. When I did it, I felt so sick I wanted to die. I still feel sick when I think about it.

I am a proud father of two great children. My daughter, Sarah, is my oldest and I have a son, John.

As a father, I want my children to obey me because I love them, and want the best for them. I know what's good for them and I want to protect them by teaching them what to do and what not to do – right from wrong, so to speak.

About five years ago, Sarah lost her mind, not literally, but she backslid from God. It got so bad that I wondered if that was really my daughter. (Thank God she is on fire for Him now.) Please understand that I'm not bringing up her past, but my past.

Has one of your children ever pushed you to the point where you only had one good nerve left and they were on it? I grounded her, punished her and nothing seemed to work.

One day, I was working in the yard when we got a call from the school. Sarah had been suspended and Roxie had to go get her from school.

Our house sits on seven acres that ends at the corner of our block and the house is on the other end.

When Roxie came around the corner, I was so mad that I outran the car. To this day, Roxie says she never slowed up as I jumped two fences and ran seven acres.

When Sarah got out of the car, I was so mad that I pulled back my fist to hit her (I have never hit one of my children like this and neither should you). The only thing that stopped me from hitting Sarah was my Roxie. I couldn't risk hitting my beloved.

Like Christ, she stood between Sarah and her father's anger at that moment. I looked at Sarah's eyes and I saw fear and it sickened me. I want my children to obey me, but not to fear me. I love her. I want her to love me. So it is with our Father.

He wants us to obey Him out of love, not fear and when He does punish us, we do not have to be dismayed.

Jesus took the blunt of it 2000 years ago on the cross. If you are led by the Spirit, even in times of rebuke, the Spirit will remind you that you are still His son or daughter.

Notice in Romans 8, we cry *"Abba Father"* the same name that Jesus cried out in the garden when His sweat became as drops of blood.

We are instructed by God in His word to cry "Abba Father" which means loving Father.

The closest English word we have is <u>Daddy</u>. We are to call Him by the same name Jesus did. Is it possible that it is because He is our Father also? Yes, we are the sons of God.

The reason the word <u>Sons of God</u> is used is

because in Israel, only a son could be an heir of God. However, in God, there is neither male nor female, Jew nor Greek or Gentile. We are all the same at the foot of the cross.

Romans 8:16 says: "*The Spirit itself beareth witness with our spirit, that we are the children of God.*" You've been adopted. In this verse Paul is writing to the Romans and according to the Roman Law of Adoption, it was as if I was born to you naturally and could not be written out of the will anytime anyone desired.

It also was to prevent people from adopting people just to make slaves out of them as most people owned family businesses and if you adopted a child, you couldn't remove them from the will. They could however, remove themselves from the will by denouncing their father.

God has never walked away from one of His children. If a man loses out with God, it is because he walked away, not God. The only way you can lose your salvation is to give up on God, because He will never give up on you.

Please notice in verse 17, it says: *"And if children, then heirs; heirs of God, and joint-heirs with Christ; if so be that we suffer with Him, that we may be also glorified together."* Do you see that? God will disappoint you so you will grow because you can't receive your inheritance until you are of age. As you grow and can handle it, you will receive more and more of the inheritance – literally all that is Christ's is available to you.

Because of this, I will not fear or want, for He who spared not His Son, how much more through Him will He freely give us all things?

I will not fear that He loves me *For God so loved the world that He gave His only begotten Son.*

I will not fear the devil *For the God of peace shall bruise satan under your feet shortly.*

Now what results can we expect because of His great love for us?

The Blessing
Chapter 7

Romans 8:37 says: "*Nay, in all these things we are more than conquerors through Him that loved us.*" Do you see that? We are more than conquerors because He loves us! Us, here is you and me. We can overcome anything in our lives because of the love of Christ.

I pray that you are now beginning to understand how much God truly loves us and because of that love, we can enjoy victory over all things and receive all of His blessings. Because He loves us, all we have to do is learn how to apply these blessings.

What I'm now going to share with you will change your life forever. It is all based on the love of God and us allowing God to love us and learning how to allow God to bless us.

Over the past couple of years, I have noticed an attack against not only myself, but many others in the body of Christ. Many good people, strong people of the faith have shared with me how they have gone through terrible warfare. So, I began to seek God for an answer, for a Word for myself as well as for His people and God gave me a Word.

The Word was: "*Whatsoever you bind on earth shall be bound in Heaven. Whatsoever you loose on earth, shall be loosed in Heaven.*"

You may say, John, I've done that and it is still not better. God revealed to me that a lot of us, including me, are binding things but not loosing things in their place.

The enemy attacks us to keep us under the curse. We were all born under the law of sin which basically means that because of sin, we have to live in poverty. That's part of the curse just like sickness. (The only part of us not affected by the curse is our spirit man. Our flesh and our souls are affected by the curse, however, we can invoke change by speaking blessings into those areas as you will see as this chapter progresses). When we were born again, it was from the curse to walk in blessing.

Please notice Galatians 3:13 & 14:

13.   Christ hath redeemed us from the curse of the

law, being made a curse for us: for it is written, Cursed is everyone that hangeth on a tree:

14. That the blessing of Abraham might come on the Gentiles through Jesus Christ; that we might receive the promise of the Spirit through faith.

When you got saved, Christ redeemed (paid ransom for) you and me. What did God promise Abraham? He promised victory over his enemies. He promised health, prosperity, long life and also He promised it to Abraham's seed. You may be asking how you can know it is for you. Read Galatians 3:29: *And if ye be Christ's, then are ye Abraham's seed, and heirs according to the promise.* Everything He promised, we can have.

How do we apply this blessing? It's by faith. Notice in the verse above, where it states "*that the blessing of Abraham might come on the Gentiles.*" That word <u>might</u> is the key. The blessings come on us as we apply them. That's where binding and loosing comes in.

When we were born again, our spirit man was born again. Our flesh is still the same and that is why we must be changed from glory to glory and why Jesus cleansed His disciples through the washing of the water of the Word.

Our minds are not saved yet. That's why we have to renew our minds through the Word. They are still affected by the curse, but not under the curse. That's why we bind and loose.

If I bind the spirit of poverty, but I don't speak the blessing of prosperity, I'm no longer under the curse of poverty, but I'm also not walking in the blessing either.

The purpose of binding something is to loose something in its place. This is an act of faith.

God has dealt with me on the power of the blessing. The blessing is so powerful, it is one of the reasons God warns us not to lay hands on any man suddenly. This chapter will teach you how to apply the blessings to your life. I've been doing it for a couple of years now and it really works. This chapter is a "Blessing" to you and me, from the Master.

The word <u>blessing</u> means: to ask, to invoke God's divine favor for your situation, circumstance or condition. By blessing someone or something, you are in effect invoking change. This may take place over time. *"You shall lay hands on the sick and they shall recover."*

Healing is a blessing that must be invoked. Remember the only part of you still not under the curse is your spirit man. But the spirit man can rule over the flesh and soul (mind and emotion). As you do, blessings will begin to affect your soul's realm (your flesh). You will understand better as we go along.

In the study of the four gospels, you will find that Jesus rarely cursed anything. He did curse the fig tree for not producing, He bound demons, rebuked the wind and waves and He healed the sick.

If you notice, most of the time Jesus, when confronted by a problem, spoke a blessing over it and that invoked the change. A case in point is when He fed the 5000 with five loaves and two fishes. Five loaves and two fishes will not feed 5000 and you know that and I know that (five loaves and two fishes will not feed me if

I haven't eaten in three days). It's a good thing that Jesus doesn't know that. Why do you think that they could only come up with five loaves and two fishes from a crowd that size? That is not much of an offering.

The point is; that they were under the curse of poverty. Jesus was about to show them the power of the blessing. He didn't rebuke poverty, He blessed it and it multiplied by the thousands, and *after all had eaten there was more left than when they started.*

I bless my wife and children several times a day. It is the first thing I do when I get out of bed and the last thing I do at night. The results have been amazing.

As I told you earlier in the book, Sarah had been battling a spirit of fear. I spoke the blessing of God's perfect love in her life and the fear left that day!

All of God's promises are blessings spoken by God to man so we could employ them to invoke change.

What role must we play in the blessing process? We need to speak the Word, but we also can speak our heart's desires over things.

The Old Testament patriarch's – Abraham, Isaac and Jacob, whom God changed his name to Israel as a blessing – all spoke blessings on their children and the blessings came to pass just as they said.

Jacob understood the power of the blessing to invoke change. Remember when he wrestled with God all night and God told him to let me go, but Jacob said, "*I won't let you go until you bless me.*" The blessing changed Jacob to Israel, from con man to a prince with God, which resulted in a supernatural change in his life. For now, he has power with God and man. But in order to receive this blessing, he had to wrestle all night.

Wrestling is one of the hardest sports. Two or three minutes will wear you out which is the reason why there are timed rounds in wrestling.

Jacob dislocated his hip during this wrestling match and now he was not only tired, but in great pain and still wouldn't quit. He knew once God blessed him, it would be forever. Can you imagine how tired Jacob became? Jacob was saying, "I don't care how tired or how much pain I'm in, I won't let you go until you bless me." How did he know this? Because years before Jacob had stolen his brother's blessing in Genesis 27:1-40:

> 1. And it came to pass, that when Isaac was old, and his eyes were dim, so that he could not see, he called Esau his eldest son, and said unto him, My son: and he said unto him, Behold, here am I.
>
> 2. And he said, Behold now, I am old, I know not the day of my death:
>
> 3. Now therefore take, I pray thee, thy weapons, thy quiver and thy bow, and go out to the field, and take me some venison;
>
> 4. And make me savoury meat, such as I love, and bring it to me, that I may eat; that my soul may bless thee before I die.
>
> 5. And Rebekah heard when Isaac spake to Esau his son. And Esau went to the field to hunt for venison, and to bring it.
>
> 6. And Rebekah spake unto Jacob her son, saying, Behold, I heard thy father speak unto Esau thy brother, saying,

7. Bring me venison, and make me savoury meat, that I may eat, and bless thee before the LORD before my death.

8. Now therefore, my son, obey my voice according to that which I command thee.

9. Go now to the flock, and fetch me from thence two good kids of the goats; and I will make them savoury meat for thy father, such as he loveth:

10. And thou shalt bring it to thy father, that he may eat, and that he may bless thee before his death.

11. And Jacob said to Rebekah his mother, Behold, Esau my brother is a hairy man, and I am a smooth man:

12. My father peradventure will feel me, and I shall seem to him as a deceiver; and I shall bring a curse upon me, and not a blessing.

13. And his mother said unto him, Upon me be thy curse, my son: only obey my voice, and go fetch me them.

14. And he went, and fetched, and brought them to his mother: and his mother made savoury meat, such as his father loved.

15. And Rebekah took goodly raiment of her eldest son Esau, which were with her in the house, and put them upon Jacob her younger son:

16. And she put the skins of the kids of the goats upon his hands, and upon the smooth of his neck:

17. And she gave the savoury meat and the bread, which she had prepared, into the hand of her son Jacob.

18. And he came unto his father, and said, My father: and he said, Here am I; who art thou, my son?

19. And Jacob said unto his father, I am Esau thy first born; I have done according as thou badest me: arise, I pray thee, sit and eat of my venison, that thy soul may bless me.

20. And Isaac said unto his son, How is it that thou hast found it so quickly, my son? And he said, Because the LORD thy God brought it to me.

21. And Isaac said unto Jacob, Come near, I pray thee, that I may feel thee, my son, whether thou be my very son Esau or not.

22. And Jacob went near unto Isaac his father; and

he felt him, and said, The voice is Jacob's voice, but the hands are the hands of Esau.

23. And he discerned him not, because his hands were hairy, as his brother Esau's hands: so he blessed him.

24. And he said, Art thou my very son Esau? And he said, I am.

25. And he said, Bring it near to me, and I will eat of my son's venison, that my soul may bless thee. And he brought it near to him, and he did eat: and he brought him wine and he drank.

26. And his father Isaac said unto him, Come near now, and kiss me, my son.

27. And he came near, and kissed him: and he smelled the smell of his raiment, and blessed him, and said, See, the smell of my son is as the smell of a field which the LORD hath blessed:

28. Therefore God give thee of the dew of heaven, and the fatness of the earth, and plenty of corn and wine:

29. Let people serve thee, and nations bow down to thee: be lord over thy brethren, and let thy mother's sons

bow down to thee: cursed be every one that curseth thee, and blessed be he that blesseth thee.

30. And it came to pass, as soon as Isaac had made an end of blessing Jacob, and Jacob was yet scarce gone out from the presence of Isaac his father, that Esau his brother came in from his hunting.

31. And he also had made savoury meat, and brought it unto his father, and said unto his father, Let my father arise, and eat of his son's venison, that thy soul may bless me.

32. And Isaac his father said unto him, Who art thou? And he said, I am thy son, thy firstborn Esau.

33. And Isaac trembled very exceedingly, and said, Who? where is he that hath taken venison, and brought it to me, and I have eaten of all before thou camest, and have blessed him? yea, and he shall be blessed.

34. And when Esau heard the words of his father, he cried with a great and exceeding bitter cry, and said unto his father, Bless me, even me also, O my father.

35. And he said, Thy brother came with subtilty,

and hath taken away thy blessing.

36. And he said, Is not he rightly named Jacob? for he hath supplanted me these two times: he took away my birthright; and, behold, now he hath taken away my blessing. And he said, Hast thou not reserved a blessing for me?

37. And Isaac answered and said unto Esau, Behold, I have made him thy lord, and all his brethren have I given to him for servants; and with corn and wine have I sustained him: and what shall I do now unto thee, my son?

38. And Esau said unto his father, Hast thou but one blessing, my father? bless me, even me also, O my father. And Esau lifted up his voice, and wept.

39. And Isaac his father answered and said unto him, Behold, thy dwelling shall be the fatness of the earth, and of the dew of heaven from above;

40. And by thy sword shalt thou live, and shalt serve thy brother; and it shall come to pass when thou shalt have the dominion, that thou shalt break his yoke from off thy neck.

Notice Isaac is being deceived by Jacob. Jacob lies in verse 20 and again in verse 24, but notice in verse 33, "*and have blessed him? Yea, and he shall be blessed.*" Do you see that?

Once spoken, the blessing is so powerful you cannot take it back. We need to walk in blessing to be a blessing to others.

God promised Abraham that through his seed the nations of the world would be blessed. Jesus was of his seed, but Abraham's son was born under the same curse as all men. Because Abraham had a covenant with God, he was able to bless his son and he then walked in that blessing just as he said. His blessing invoked change from curse to blessing.

It is important to remember that these men were not priests for there was no formal priesthood yet. They were not prophets and they did not even write a book of the Bible. At times they were weak; cowards, dishonest and they were humans just like you and me. They also were parents that wanted the best for their children.

We can speak blessings over our children, our

marriages, our businesses, our towns, our churches, our pastors, our country, etc. Speak the blessing opposite of your need or just bless them as to the kind of people you want them to become, the kind of mate you want them to have, God's favor in their lives, good health, wisdom, prosperity, etc.

It's easy to bless the ones you love, but Jesus also said to bless your enemies. You may ask, "Why would I do that?" I'll give you a few reasons.

First, it makes you like Him. He blesses those who don't deserve it.

Second, it says "I trust You, God." God is big on trust. "I trust You God that You can protect me more than my enemies can harm me, so I bless them." Bless them and they may get saved as you bless them.

God bless them and they will realize it's because of you. It's called heaping coals of fire on their heads. But the most important reason of all is because you are a child of God and when you are under attack, God defends His children as you or I would defend our children.

God is saying, "bless them, hold me back or I'll have to wake them up." Your blessing stops the wrath of God on them.

Now, let us look at six powerful verses on the blessing. I started speaking this blessing over my family about a year ago, but I only knew in part and the results in my family were just unbelievable. These six verses do not cover the power of the blessing, but it should give you an idea or prototype. It does not limit you to these six verses. It will reveal how the blessing is to be pronounced and what God does when we bless someone and how God blesses them.

Pronouncing The Blessing
Chapter 8

Numbers 6:22-27 says:

22. And the LORD spake unto Moses, saying,

23. Speak unto Aaron and unto his sons, saying, On this wise ye shall bless the children of Israel, saying unto them,

24. The LORD bless thee, and keep thee:

25. The LORD make his face shine upon thee, and be gracious unto thee:

26. The LORD lift up his countenance upon thee, and give thee peace.

27. And they shall put my name upon the children of Israel, and I will bless them.

First notice verses 22 and 23. The Lord said to do this. The blessing is God's idea. He also has commanded me to bless you with this book.

Now let's do a word study in the Hebrew. Verse 24 says: "*The LORD bless thee, and keep thee.*" Blessings one and two are in this verse. The word <u>bless</u> in the Hebrew means <u>barak</u>. It means to bow in adoration and to worship God with great affection and passion and as you do this, it blesses God, but it doesn't end there and vise-versa.

What He is saying is that He will make you the object of His affections. The first blessing is God's passionate affection.

Speak a blessing on that child on drugs, the child in jail, in sin and when you do, they will become the object of God's affection. All three times, <u>bless</u> appears in these verses it is the word <u>barak</u>.

In over 80% of the Old Testament, the word <u>bless</u> is <u>barak</u>. God's affection would be enough, but there is more, a lot more. The love of God is the driving force behind the blessing.

Before I go any further, let me remind you that these are the children of Israel, a rebellious people, stiff necked, fornicators, and at times idolaters. This will bless you. Even though they were not perfect, they were the people of promise. To possess the land, the blessing invoked change in these people so God could give them the Promised Land.

Blessing number two is the word, <u>keep</u>. Oh, beloved, I wonder what would happen if I could find the time to study the Bible word by word? The English language just doesn't do the Hebrew or Greek justice.

The word, <u>keep</u> means; that God is a hedge about you because you are the object of His affection. It means; to protect you because He is a watchman over you and it means; to keep you safe and sure because you are the object of His affection.

Hold on, it gets even better. Blessings three, four and five are all found in verse 25. "*The LORD make His face shine upon thee, and be gracious unto thee.*"

The word, <u>face</u> means; that when His face is on you, His favor and His protection are on you, implying how His eyes always are on you to protect you. It also means; He is pleased with you and it shows in His face.

Now let's look at the word <u>shine</u>. I speak these verses over my family at least twice a day. The word, <u>shine</u> means; to make luminous like the faces of Moses and Stephen. It means; a glorious shining that causes you to be set on fire, to burse into flames. Don't worry, that which is natural is natural and that which is spiritual is spiritual. It means His blessing produces a passion for Him, for life.

John the Baptist said, *"I indeed baptize you with water into repentance, but He that cometh after me is mightier than I whose shoes I am not worthy to latch and He shall baptize you with the Holy Ghost and fire."*

The word <u>fire</u> means; passion, to be passionately in love with God and He with me. It also means; to shine as in smiling at someone.

The word <u>gracious</u> (I hope this is blessing you as much as it is me to write), means; to bend, to stoop down in kindness to one who is inferior and as you do, you bestow great mercy. It means; to have pity on, but never in a condescending way.

Blessings six, seven, eight and nine are all

found in verse 26 which reads "*The LORD lift up His countenance upon thee, and give thee peace.*" There is so much here in just three verses.

Here in verse 26, we discover how the entire Godhead is involved in the blessing. God the Father, God the Son and God the Holy Ghost.

Before I go into the blessings of verse 26, the word here is YAH-WEH and this is very important. For it tells us who makes this blessing available and how He makes this blessing available. YAH-WEH is the name for God that identifies him as Israel's covenant God.

What does this name mean? Folks, this is powerful, so please pay close attention. In Genesis chapter one, God introduces Himself to mankind as ELOHIM which means; all powerful, all mighty, all everything!

This name by itself is only used in acts of power and yes greatness, but only in acts and never in relationship. It presents God, but only presents who God is.

In Genesis 2:4-8 we receive the second revelation of God:

4. These are the generations of the heavens and of the earth when they were created, in the day that the LORD God made the earth and the heavens.

5. And every plant of the field before it was in the earth and every herb of the field before it grew: for the LORD God had not caused it to rain upon the earth and there was not a man to till the ground.

6. But there went up a mist from the earth, and watered the whole face of the ground.

7. And the LORD God formed man of the dust of the ground, and breathed into his nostrils the breath of life; and man became a living soul.

8. And the LORD God planted a garden eastward in Eden; and there He put the man whom He had formed.

God gives a revelation of Himself to mankind. Here He introduces Himself as JEHOVAH-ELOHIM. Why this new revelation? Because now God is creating man to have fellowship with Him, a relationship with Him, so now it is JEHOVAH-ELOHIM. JEHOVAH is the name of God connected to covenant relationship.

Notice He is still all powerful and all mighty, but He put covenant before His power, relationship before His authority.

The name JEHOVAH is only used in connection with relationship. Every time the word LORD appears in the blessing, it is the word YAHWEH which is these two names together, both titles in one word with something extra at the end. The eternal God.

The word, <u>eternal</u> means; He is in the past, the present and the future all at the same time. Do you see why He is the author and finisher of your faith? He knows the end before the beginning. He is at the end of your life already; He's in your tomorrow already so you have nothing to fear.

This name is just like Jesus in Revelation when He declares He is the beginning and the end – the Alpha and Omega. In fact, this is Jesus. Let me explain. It is Jesus on the cross who pays for the covenant, making it available to all. He is the power of the covenant. This is thrilling.

When God spoke to Moses through the burning bush concerning their deliverance from Egypt, Moses said he tried once in his own strength and it didn't work. What if they run me off again? Who should I say sent me? God replies: "*Tell them YAHWEH (I am that I am) sent you.*" God makes us a lot of promises in connection to the covenant.

YAHWEH is the name used by God to reveal the delivering power of the covenant. This name always deals with the power of God being manifested for those in the covenant to bring them out. Now all the power, might and wisdom of God is at work to bring the covenant to pass in your life as you apply it by faith. One of the ways to apply it is to pronounce the blessing.

Jesus, which means; JEHOVAH, saves with total salvation of the body, soul and spirit.

When Jesus was in His earthly walk they asked Him, "*By what authority do you do these miracles?*" He said "*I am that I am. I am YAHWEH.*" That's why they tried to stone Him.

YAHWEH is the name used by God to bring men out. It is the power of the covenant to purpose redemption of body, soul and spirit. He is the great I am.

When Jesus died and then rose from the dead, He declared all power has been given to me in Heaven and in earth. He has all power.

The name YAHWEH always deals with the power of the covenant to bring people out.

Jesus died on the cross to make the covenant available. He rose with all power so when we speak the blessing using His name, the power of God goes to work invoking the change.

Now that we know the power of the blessing, let's continue in teaching on the blessing.

The next words I want to teach you about are *"the LORD lift up His countenance upon thee and give thee peace."*

The word, <u>lift</u> means; to accept you, to advance you, to exalt you by forgiving you; to help you by holding you up and goes on to say how: by marrying you, by divine pardon because He regards what you ask for, or bless. Why? Because He respects you.

All that is left now is the word <u>countenance</u>. It is the same word as <u>face</u> earlier. It means; you have His favor, protection, His acceptance and implies that His eyes always are on you because He can't take His eyes off you. You are the object of His affection. It also means; He is pleased with you.

The word <u>give</u> will blow you away. It is only used three times in this manner in the whole Bible. The word <u>give</u>, appears many times, but the Hebrew word translated <u>give</u>, only appears three times because it is not just an action, but a person of action.

It means; to appoint someone to care for you, to give to you, to order your steps, to preserve you until this blessing comes to pass. This is the work of the Holy Ghost. This is what the Holy Ghost does.

When you bless someone, the word <u>peace</u> means; to be safe, to make complete, and to be friends with you. Because of this, He gives you peace by making amends for you, to perfect you for the purpose of prospering you.

In this one word, we have protection, forgiveness, atonement, a character change resulting in prosperity. Now we are about to learn the role the Father plays in the blessing.

Verse 27 of the opening portion of scripture says: "*And they shall put my name upon the children of Israel and I will bless them.*"

The word <u>name</u> here means: His name is an eternal memorial upon that person (that's why you lay hands on no man suddenly because it is eternal).

The act of blessing someone has eternal effects. That implies the power of My name, the creative power of My name, the authority of My name, the character of My name.

The closest English word we have for it is to be <u>Knighted</u>. You can now act for the Kingdom. "*Whatsoever you bind on earth is bound in Heaven; whatsoever you loose on earth is loosed in Heaven.*"

Why? Because, His name is on you. You have name recognition in Heaven. You have clout in Heaven.

Now notice the end of the verse where it says; "*put my name on them.*" In the New Testament what is the only name we are told to pray in? Jesus.

Example: "*In My name they shall cast out devils…*" Also, "*ask anything in my name.*" "*Bless them using my name*" in this verse "*and I will bring it to pass.*"

But look how He does it. *Put my name on them and I will barak (or bless) them. I will make them the object of My affection.* Do you see that. It literally means that I love them with the same love that I love whose name is on them. This is the Father loving us like his son Jesus.

The blessing is one thing, but what makes it so wonderful, is how He loves us into prosperity, loves us to victory and loves us to healing.

You may be saying, oh Brother John, they were priests and we're not or God told them to. Well, God told me to write this book to bless you.

Do we have the authority to speak the blessing? We will find out in the next chapter.

Taking Control
Chapter 9

There is only one authority that can tell us if we can bless things like the priest did. The Word. What does the Word say?

Revelation 5:8-10 says:

8. And when he had taken the book, the four beasts and four and twenty elders fell down before the Lamb, having everyone of them harps, and golden vials full of odours, which are the prayers of saints.

9. And they sung a new song, saying, Thou art worthy to take the book, and to open the seals thereof: for thou was slain, and hast redeemed us to God by thy blood out of every kindred, and tongue, and people, and nation;

10. And hast made us unto our God kings and priests: and we shall reign on the earth.

Please notice the word <u>hast</u> in verse 9. Hast is past tense. Continuing on, we see the phrase, *"redeemed us to God"* from being a slave to the evil one, to a child of

God. You see He has already redeemed us on the cross through His blood. He's done His part and we must now do our part.

Verse 10 says: *"And hast* (Jesus has already) *made us unto our God kings and priests; and we shall reign on the earth."* Kings rule.

The problem is the earth we are on is cursed through sin. That is why there will have to be a new Heaven and a new earth so we will rule as kings in all things that pertain to us such as our family, our health, etc.

The environment is covered by sin and we are surrounded by sin. But notice, Jesus also made us priests. Before I go further into this, why did He make us kings and priests? So we can reign on the earth. Kings rule.

Priests primarily made sacrifices. We don't do that because Jesus was the final sacrifice. He paid the debt in full so now all we have to do is offer the sacrifice of praise. The priests also blessed the people as in Numbers chapter 6. As kings, we rule, as priests, we can invoke change in our kingdom or environment by speaking a blessing.

Starting now, take control by speaking blessings and watch God invoke change in all that you bless.

It's For You!
Chapter 10

While writing this book, I continued learning even more about God's incredible love. Even after over 26 years of ministry, I am still learning more about the love of Christ; it is truly measureless. This is a subject that I never grow tired of studying and I am amazed at how with each rewrite, God would reveal more and more thrilling truths to me about his awesome love. Beloved, I am amazed at how He created us to love us, and we were created to love Him. It is only in this relationship that we find true fulfillment. So many people seek for fulfillment through other means and never find it. Your family, spouse, and friends are gifts from God and should be enjoyed and appreciated, but only God's love can totally fulfill you.
I'm sure by now you may be wondering how you can experience the fullness of that love in my own life. While thinking and praying about how to close this book, I began to ask myself how I could possibly sum up what it is that I've been sharing with you about the marvelous love of Christ. I believe the Holy Spirit spoke to me as clear as a bell, simply, the plan of Salvation, God's single greatest expression of love.

> For God so loved that world, that he gave His only begotten Son, that whosoever believeth in Him should not perish, but have everlasting life. (John 3:16 KJV)

Now, if that isn't love, I don't know what is. The Father loved us so much that He willingly gave His Son for us. The Son loved us so much that He willingly laid down His life for us. Now that's love!

At this point, some of you are probably thinking, "Brother John, I'm already saved, but I'm still not experiencing the fullness of what you've been describing." Yes, you are saved and so am I, which makes you a child of God. However, Salvation, the act of Salvation (initial conversion) is only the beginning of your walk with God. That's the best part! Forgiveness of Sin, deliverance from Hell, getting to go to heaven, inheriting eternal life, answered prayers, and all of the wonderful things a person receives when they become born again, is only a small part of Salvation. It's only the beginning. You see, I believe that God is taking His church, the truly hungry ones, to a whole new level. This is not a new level for Him, but it is new for us. It is a place where we truly understand what it is to be the adopted child of God. Really, it was His plan from the very beginning. And I believe the purpose of this book has been to share that with you.

First of all, to operate in this new level of authority, we must realize who we are in Christ and how God operates in us. I believe that He operates in us and through us by relationship. You see, most of us, if not all of us, know that God is almighty, all powerful, etc. In fact, Scripture tells us that God is more powerful than we are even able to comprehend.

> Now unto Him that is able to do exceedingly abundantly above all that we ask or think, according to the power that worketh in us [.] (Eph. 3:20 KJV)

Neither the most creative or brilliant person that has ever walked the earth was able to comprehend or imagine something greater than what God is able to do for us. This means that literally nothing that you or I could ever pray is beyond God's ability to accomplish. It also means that no matter how smart I am, I could never be able to comprehend the enormity of God's power. We don't fully understand His power. His power, glory, and love are beyond us. But we believe it. We know that there are no limits with God and yet we often wonder why we don't see more of His power manifested in our lives. Often our problem is that we have trouble operating in God's delegated authority. Even though we realize the power, authority, and love that is available to us, we simply don't feel worthy of God doing these great things in our personal lives. The problem is that we know He can do these things, but we question whether He wants to do them. Sometimes we even assume God will do things for other people, but He may not do them for us. It often goes like this, someone believes that God would do great things for their Pastor, or Brother John, or other people that she may admire or look up to, but she doesn't think that He can do these things in her life. In this way, we are dysfunctional. The Body of Christ, in many places, is dysfunctional because we realize who God is, but we do not realize who we are in Him.

So, who are we really in God? I believe that the Word of God answers this best in Ephesians chapter 1 verses 1-5.

> Paul, an apostle of Jesus Christ by the will of God, to the saints which are at Ephesus, and to the faithful in Christ Jesus [.]
> (Eph. 1:1 KJV)

I'm John, an Evangelist of my Lord Jesus Christ, by the will of God. I'm not bragging on me in saying this. I'm just saying that what I am about to say is not from me, but from God. First of all, I believe God placed this in my heart as a specific Word in Season. Secondly, as it is from the Bible, it is always profitable. "Heaven and earth shall pass away, but my words shall not pass away" (Matt. 24:35 KJV). Notice, the end of verse one, "to the faithful in Christ Jesus". Are you living for God? Do you know Him in relationship? Than this is certainly for you!

> Grace be to you, and peace, from God our Father, and from the Lord Jesus Christ. (Eph. 1:2 KJV)

God's grace produces peace in our lives, not fear or dread. This grace comes from God *our* Father and *our* Lord Jesus Christ. Folks this is awesome! God is saying, I'm your Father and you're my child. Let that sink into your heart for a minute. That is what happened when you accepted Christ as Savior. The word "grace" (cariv// charis) here is very powerful. It means both *to* us and *in* us. To us, it means unmerited favor. The word favor means to be pursued by God's glory for the purpose of blessing. This is why God pursued you in the first place, to bless you. It means that because of what Jesus did for me on the Cross, although I don't deserve any of God's blessings, by His Word, they are *all* mine anyhow because of God's grace.

The second part of the definition for grace means God's ability and power to do it. Beloved, I don't live for God by my own power, but by His. I don't receive His blessings by my power either, nor can I. I must receive God's blessings by His power. Can He do it? Of course He can? But will He? Grace says He will. Thank you

Jesus!

> Blessed be the God and Father of our Lord Jesus Christ, who hath blessed us with all spiritual blessings in heavenly places in Christ [.] (Eph. 1:3 KJV)

The word "blessed" here has the same meaning as chapter 8 and 9. We need to bless God through worship for all He has done for us. When we do, He "inhabits the praises of His people," and because of that there is a sense of love, joy, and peace. We should worship Him for many reasons.

The tense of this passage is important here. It says "who hath blessed us with all spiritual blessings". This is in past tense. He has already done this. We must remember that God has already given me *all* His spiritual blessings. It's a done deal. Of most importance is the word "all". Not most, not some, but *all* blessings, every promise in the Bible belongs to you and me through Christ Jesus. Some spiritual blessings are love, joy, peace, the gifts of the Spirit, answered prayer. In short, all God possesses, He has already given to you. Some may be asking, "Brother, if this is so, why don't I enjoy these benefits?" Notice the answer right here in this verse. These blessings exist in "heavenly places". In other words, they are not natural, but spiritual. Miracles can be produced in the natural, but the source of the miracles is spiritual. If we want these blessings, we have to go up, not so much like in space, but expand in our relationship with Christ. How do I know this? Notice how we go up, "in Christ". The heavenly place we must reach is in Him. You see, we must go up and in, up to heavenly places by going deeper in Christ. As we do, these blessings manifest in our lives automatically.

To rise up in heavenly places may seem more complicated than it actually is. You see, to go deeper in Christ we must simply be hungry for God and seek Him through prayer, worship, and study. It is a spiritual place and I have learned that you can only operate in the Kingdom from the Kingdom.

> According as he hath chosen us in him before the foundation of the world, that we should be holy and without blame before him in love [.] (Eph. 1:4 KJV)

First of all, you need to know that you are special. God *chose you*, hand-picked you. Again, we are in the past tense here, which means that he has already done it. Notice now that He chose you, "before the foundation of the world". Now this is truly mind-boggling. Before God made anything, even the earth we stand on, He chose you to be part of His family. Do you see how special you are to God? As a father, I had to supply a home for my children and wife to live. Furthermore,

Roxie and I tried to make it a pleasant environment for them. We remodeled to make our home more safe and enjoyable for our children. Outside, we made a small play ground, a pool to swim in, and a pond to fish in. We planted flowers and flowering shrubs. By now, I'm sure you're getting the picture. All God has created was *for* you and I. He knew us before He made any of it, and He made it with us in mind. In fact, He made it for us to live in. Now that's awesome! Everything God made was a home for His children. All of His wonderful creation is for us, His family, to live in. Wow!

Now notice that because of this, we should be holy and without blame before Him in love. As we feast on God's love, He makes us holy and blameless. Now, I feel I must pause to explain something here. Only God can make us Holy. I couldn't save myself. Nor can I keep myself saved. It is only God working in me that brings this to pass. Because of His working in me, I'm blameless before Him in love. He does this simply because He loves me, and I gave my life to Him. So, I am blameless. You may wonder, "How is that possible"? First of all, when I got saved, He forgot all my sins and cleansed me of all unrighteousness. When you and I became Christians, He removed all our sins, replaced them with the righteousness of Jesus, who is sinless, blameless. The Bible says that He imputed onto us His righteousness. I'm righteous because God says I am, and all of this is because of Jesus. I must add here that it really isn't hard to be faithful when you really love the one you're in the relationship with. As we live in God's love, we find it much easier to live for Him.

> Having predestinated us unto the adoption of children by Jesus Christ to himself, according to the good pleasure of his will [.] (Eph. 1:5 KJV)

First of all, we must realize that Jesus always was; He is eternal. In other words, He existed in eternity before He became flesh on earth. He exists in the past, present and future simultaneously. When Jesus was in His earth walk, He only existed in the present and was limited as we are in time. Then, He died and rose from the dead. When He did, He entered the eternal again, where He is now. I don't want to suggest a type of Calvinism. I do not believe that God chose some to be saved and others to be lost. I can say this with confidence because I know my God. I know that He loved the world so much that He gave His only begotten Son so that all could be saved. He desires that none should perish, but that all should come to eternal life. God's Word is also clear that Christ died for the sins of the whole world. He didn't take yours and leave mine, or vice-versa. I believe God, who is eternal, created the plan of Salvation before the foundation of the world. But we choose by our own free will if we will accept that plan. Of course, God, who is in the past, present and future all at the same time, could know who would chose and who would not. I believe He chooses not to know. Anyway, I can say with confidence that no man was born to go to hell. It's a choice that we all make. Having said that, notice what He has predestined for you and me, adoption. The great news is that we are not orphans; we are adopted children.

Out of all the people that have ever lived, He chose us. Why? For many reasons. Remember that word "Barak," which means to adore someone. Well, God adores you, and He chose you for adoption because He adores you. You're adorable! In my case, He didn't pick the smartest, prettiest, or even nicest person. No, He picked a broken, drug addict and said, "I want that one with all His flaws. I adore Him." You see, we're not orphans, but children, adopted children of the most High God.

In my travels, I've ministered to orphans. I've noticed that they often eat too much and they often steal from each other. If you back a truck full of toys up to the place where they are, they will fight over just one toy. Why do they do this? Is it because they are bad children? No! It's because they're dysfunctional. They don't have parents, so in their sweet little minds, they don't know where the next meal is coming from or if there will even be one. They don't sense a father or mother's care, so they feel they must take care of themselves. However, I've seen some of these children adopted. Often, they act the same way at first because they don't realize who they are to their new parents. But sooner or later, it begins to sink in that they have parents now who will provide for them. Often, they start giving stuff away because they know what it is like to be without. It wasn't that they lacked character, they were just scared. All too often, I see this type of behavior in the church. People are afraid to give and share because they have an orphan mentality. But when you realize the Father is your source, you give, knowing He will take care of you. Beloved, we're in the big time! I'm adopted by the Father, I'm going to marry the Son. We are truly members of God's family!

My brother Ray and his wife Sue have two adopted children and they are as much of a family as any could be. I've noticed some interesting things about them that I would like to share with you. First of all, they look like their parents. I have heard people say that and had my doubts thinking, "Are you nuts? They're adopted." But at the 2008 Christmas party, I was standing back; looking at all four of them together, and I found myself saying, "Hey, they do look alike." So it is with the Father. As we live in His love, from glory to glory, encounter to encounter, we begin to look and act like Him.

I can remember how before the adoption went through, how excited Ray and Sue were about the adoption. I also remember how broken-hearted they were when a few of them fell through. I imagine that God the Father feels the same heart break when someone rejects His gift of Salvation. They loved the child before it was even born. They told me all their plans for the child, showed me the presents they had bought them, and showed me the baby's room that they had decorated in preparation for the new child. All of this before they ever knew if they were even going to get the child. This is why they were adopting in the first place. Ray and Sue are two of the best parents I have ever known. Even before they had children, they desired children because they had a lot to share and a desire to care for a child. They had money, a home, wisdom, talents, but they had no one to share that with, until they adopted.

So it is with our Father. He owns it all, but He had no one to share it with. He has all the wonderful knowledge, and He wanted children to share it with. He wanted children to care for, to provide for, protect, love and adore. You see, what good is it to have it all and no one to share it with? God, your Father and mine, adopted us to share with us all He has, and He did this through the Father/child relationship. He had a Son and He gave Him, so He could have many sons and daughters. By Christ Jesus and what He did for us on the Cross, in accordance with the good pleasures of His will, we are God's family. The plan of Salvation, or Divine adoption, is the good pleasure of the Father's will.

> But rather seek ye the kingdom of God; and all these things shall be added unto you. Fear not, little flock; for it is your Father's good pleasure to give you the kingdom.
>
> (Luke 12:31-2 KJV)

This chapter in Luke deals with people worrying about how they're going to make it, or "get by". Jesus is teaching here that the Father of Heaven cares too. So, He sent Jesus. The reason Jesus came is because man was cut off from God because of sin. On the Cross, He would pay the price for that sin. You see, the Cross was the bridge between heaven and earth, God and man. And because of what Jesus did on the Cross, you can be adopted by God, be a part of the royal family. God wants to be your Father. That is what Salvation is all about. God wants to share all He has with me and you.

Jesus says in verse 31, if your God's child by your own freewill, you chose to be adopted. If you did, than life is simple. "Seek ye first the Kingdom of God; and all these things shall be added unto you". The word "seek" here means to spend time with the Father. He will instruct you through His Word, by His Spirit. He has great plans for you. He has things to share with you, but you'll never know it or receive it unless you spend time with Him. It comes from Him. All of His blessings come through Jesus.

Now, notice verse 32. "Fear not little flock." This certainly resonates with all the world's problems today. The word "flock" here could mean family. The use of flock implies the presence of a shepherd. Of course, we know that Jesus is the good shepherd of God's flock, or family. If we follow Him, we will be ok. He protects, provides, heals and feeds us. The Father and Son work together to care for us, Their family. If we will seek Him and follow Him, look what He has for us! For it is *your* Father's good pleasure to give you the Kingdom. Do you see that? He's *your* Father and He wants to give you the Kingdom! That's why He adopted you, to give you all that He has, and He has a lot to give. In fact, He has more than you could ever need or even dream of asking. If you haven't asked Christ into your heart, won't you do it now? Simply ask Him to forgive your sins. Ask

Him into your heart as your Lord and Savior, and if you do, the Father will adopt you this very moment. If you just did that, welcome to the family of God! If you are already a Christian, seek the Father, spend time with Him. Feast on His love and the love the of the Son, and a whole new world will be yours, now and forever. Amen.

A Special Thank You

I would like to express a special thanks to Roxanne, Sarah and John – my family, whose love over the years has overwhelmed my life with joy and fulfillment.

Without them, I could never have written this book because their love for me has revealed God's love for me through them.

Thank you family,

Love Dad